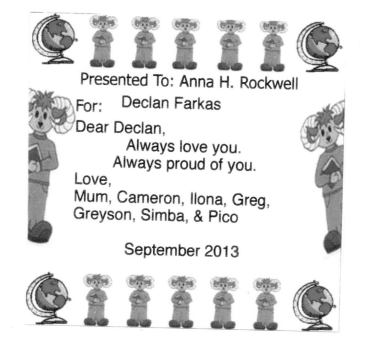

Presented To: Anna H. Rockwell

For: Declan Farkas

Dear Declan,
        Always love you.
        Always proud of you.
Love,
Mum, Cameron, Ilona, Greg,
Greyson, Simba, & Pico

September 2013

WEIRD-BUT-TRUE FACTS ABOUT GROSS THINGS

BY LAUREN COSS • ILLUSTRATED BY MERNIE GALLAGHER-COLE

The Child's World®

Published by The Child's World®
1980 Lookout Drive • Mankato, MN 56003-1705
800-599-READ • www.childsworld.com

Acknowledgments
The Child's World®: Mary Berendes, Publishing Director
Red Line Editorial: Editorial direction
The Design Lab: Design
Amnet: Production

ISBN 9781614734147
LCCN 2012946521

Printed in the United States of America
Mankato, MN
November, 2012
PA02143

About the Author

Lauren Coss is an author and editor living in Saint Paul, Minnesota. After writing this book, she decided to buy a new pillow.

About the Illustrator

A former greeting card artist, Mernie Gallagher-Cole is a freelance illustrator with over 28 years experience illustrating for children. Her charming illustrations can be found on greeting cards, party goods, games, puzzles, children's books, and now e-books and educational game apps! She lives in Philadelphia with her husband and two children.

TABLE OF CONTENTS

INTRODUCTION

From toilets to termites, the world can be a stinky, slimy, and downright disgusting place. Do you know what your feet and stinky cheese have in common? Get ready to meet the creatures you share your pillow with every night. It's time to check out the grosser side of things. And remember, even though these facts might seem too weird and revolting to be real, they are all true!

4FT

CREEPY CRAWLIES

Maggots are one of the best ways to treat an infection.

These baby flies are so efficient at cleaning wounds, some modern hospitals use them to treat wounds and stomach ulcers. The flies eat the dead tissue deep in wounds that can get infected.

It's legal for maggots to swim in your orange juice.

According to the U.S. Food and Drug Administration, 1 cup (.2 L) of orange juice can have two maggots. Ten fly eggs are also permitted in each cup. These crawlies are so small you would not ordinarily notice them.

The giant Gippsland earthworm can grow up to 10 feet (3 m) long.

These slimy creatures burrow deep in the ground in the state of Victoria, Australia. Another strange worm is the North Auckland worm of New Zealand. These weird worms can grow to be 30 inches (75 cm) long and are fuzzy and **bioluminescent**, meaning they glow in the dark.

Leeches can drink up to eight times their body weight in blood.

They are so efficient that some hospitals use them during surgeries. A leech's spit has blood thinner in it that helps keep blood from thickening.

Millipedes stink.

Most types of millipedes have stink glands. When threatened, a millipede curls into a ball and gives off a smelly, poisonous liquid. The stinky poison can make animals sick or even die if they make the mistake of eating the millipede.

Flies spit on their food before they eat it.

Housefly saliva has special chemicals to help break down solid food. When the fly spits on the solid food, it turns into a liquid so the fly can suck it up.

A tapeworm can lay 100,000 eggs in one human every day.

Tapeworms live inside the guts of animals and humans. An adult tapeworm can live up to 25 years and grow to be longer than a school bus.

ANIMAL LEAVINGS

Billy goats urinate on their own beards.

This lets female goats know the males are interested in them and attracts the females to them.

When a vulture is scared, it pukes on its attacker.

The vomit lets the vulture lose some of its body weight so it can escape faster. The vomit is usually poisonous and can harm or kill some animals.

Houseflies go to the bathroom every four to five minutes.

FLY RESTROOM

When attacked, a hagfish can produce up to 17 pints (8 L) of slimy mucus at a time.

The slime spreads out in the water, choking the attacking fish. The eating habits of the hagfish are just as gross as its defense. The hagfish enters a dead animal and eats it from the inside out.

An average elephant dropping can weigh up to 5 pounds (2.3 kg).

An elephant can produce up to 30 of these hefty dung balls each day.

One of the smelliest animals on Earth is the African striped polecat.

When it is attacked, a striped polecat will often spray its attacker with a liquid from its behind, much like a skunk—only smellier. The stinky animal can be smelled from a distance of seven football fields.

Termite farts produce 4 percent of the world's methane emissions.

Termites can use their farts to stop their enemies.

A termite can pass so much gas that its abdomen explodes. The guts and gases from the termite hurt or kill the intruder. The exploding termite eventually dies, but it can help keep the termite colony safe.

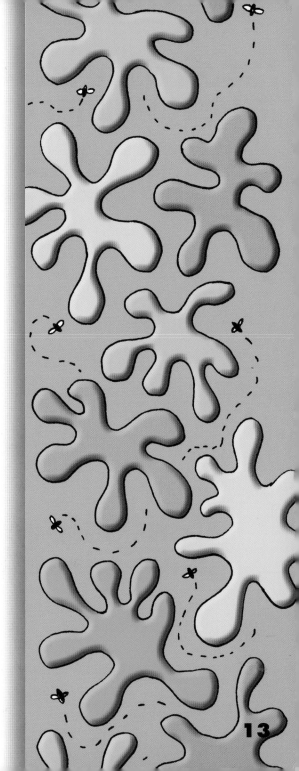

Cow dung was once used to treat wounds and sores.

In England in the 1800s, a mixture including warm cow dung was sometimes spread over injuries. Sheep and pig dung was also used to treat medical problems.

Cows pass gas every minute.

This comes in the form of both burps and farts.

Tree sloths can store poop for up to a week at a time.

During the dry season, pooping attracts predators, so sloths leave their trees to go to the bathroom. They try to do this as little as possible because they are in greater danger on the ground. When it finally goes, a sloth can poop one-fifth of its body weight. During the rainy season, sloths don't have to leave their trees because the rain will hide the smell from predators.

Rats can't burp.

They also can't throw up. Instead, they have excellent senses to help them avoid poisonous foods.

DISGUSTING HUMANS

On average, each person releases enough gas every day to fill one and one-third soda cans.

A dirty beard can smell like an armpit.

The same bacteria live in a beard that live in an armpit. Because of this, an unwashed beard can stink like body odor.

On a hot day, the average person can sweat enough in one hour to fill a coffee pot.

Most people can sweat up to 13 cups (3 l) in one hour in hot, humid conditions.

A human sheds more than 8 pounds (3.6 kg) of skin each year.

Where does it all go? Look under your bed. The dust bunnies you see are made up of mostly dead skin.

The longest fingernails in the world totaled nearly 29 feet (7.5 m).

They belonged to Lee Redmond. The longest nail was her thumb at 31.5 inches (80 cm). She broke the world's longest nails in a car accident in 2009 and does not plan to grow them out again.

Your mouth has more bacteria than there are people on Earth— more than 7 billion.

The warm, dark, moist climate of your mouth is a perfect environment for bacteria.

In 1977, a 13-year-old boy discovered a tooth growing out of his foot.

His doctor pulled out the tooth, and the boy went on to live a normal life. Doctors said the condition was extremely rare.

Frenchman Michel Lotito once ate an entire airplane.

It took him two years to finish the Cessna 150, one part at a time, but he survived the meal. He was also famous for eating bicycles, television sets, shopping carts, and more. Lotito started eating metal when he was nine years old and continued his unusual diet until he died in 2007 at age 57.

You get a new stomach lining every three days.

The human stomach is full of strong acid. The cells in the stomach's lining are replaced constantly to keep rest of the body safe.

An average human produces 2 cups (.5 liters) of mucus each day.

Your body carries enough bacteria to fill a soup can— up to 5 pounds (2.3 kg).

Most of these bacteria are helpful to you. They help keep your body working as it should. Every so often, though, unhealthy bacteria can make you sick.

Human feet can produce more than 2 cups (.5 L) of sweat each day.

Bacteria love warm, dark, moist places—like inside your shoe or sock. They also eat sweat. After they eat your sweat, they give off the stinky waste that leads to smelly feet.

The loudest burp ever recorded was almost as loud as a chainsaw.

In 2009, Englishman Paul Hunn let out the 109.9 decibel belch.

Unofficially, the distance record for human projectile vomiting is 27 feet (8.2 m).

There is no official record because you can't usually predict when it will happen!

In a typical human body, only one in ten cells are actually human.

The rest are made up of **microbes**. The microbes are tiny one-celled animals that make their homes inside humans.

GROSS GOODS AND TOILET TRIVIA

Limburger cheese smells like feet.

The bacteria that helps make the cheese is very similar to the bacteria that dines on your foot sweat. Limburger cheese is considered one of the smelliest cheeses in the world and is now only made by one company in Wisconsin.

In a 2009 survey, one in five swimmers admitted to peeing in a public pool.

One out of three swimmers admitted to not showering before jumping in.

Until recently, the biggest moneymaker on the South Pacific Island of Nauru was ancient bird poop.

The 1,000-year-old dung gives off **phosphate**, which is mined for fertilizer.

For a time, ancient Romans used human urine as an ingredient in their toothpaste.

Some lipstick contains fish scales.

The ground-up scales help make the lipstick shiny.

Gas pumps and mailbox handles are some of the dirtiest surfaces in the United States.

According to a 2011 study, these two public surfaces had the most bacteria that could make a person sick.

Up to one-third the weight of an average used pillow is made up of dust, dead skin, mites, and mite feces.

Books can get lice.

These tiny, wingless bugs eat mold or fungi growing in a book's pages. They can also live in potted plants, behind wallpaper, and in other places in your house.

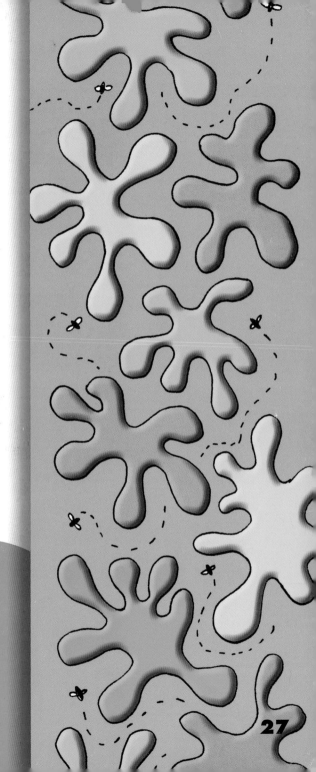

Queen Elizabeth I had a flushing toilet.

Sir John Harrington invented the flush toilet in the 1590s. As a result, a flush toilet was installed in the queen's Richmond Palace around 1596. They did not become common until the 1800s.

If you flush the toilet with the lid up, you might be getting gross bacteria on your toothbrush.

Every time you flush, bacteria from the toilet water sprays in the air. If you store your toothbrush near the toilet, toilet bacteria might end up on its bristles.

Leave It to Beaver showed the first toilet on television in 1957.

Because of strict **censorship**, the episode could only show the toilet tank. No part of the seat was visible. A toilet flush was heard on television for the first time in a 1971 episode of *All In the Family*.

The Pentagon uses an average of 666 rolls of toilet paper every day.

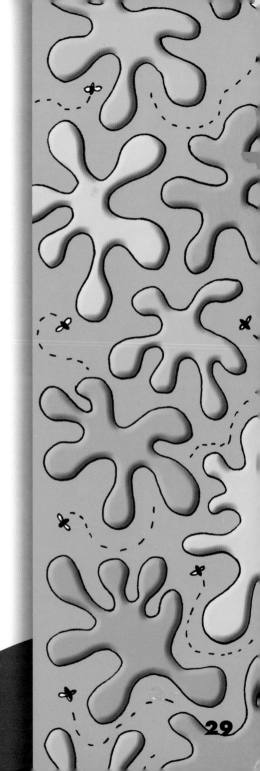

29

GLOSSARY

bioluminescent (bye-oh-loo-meh-NEH-sent)
A living thing that glows is bioluminescent. Some worms in New Zealand are bioluminescent.

censorship (SEN-sur-ship)
Censorship requires a book or movie to remove parts that are thought to be inappropriate. Censorship in television's early days prevented toilets from appearing on television shows.

infection (in-FEK-shuhn)
An infection is a sickness caused by viruses or bacteria. Some hospitals use maggots to help prevent or treat an infection.

maggots (MAG-uhtz)
Maggots are young flies. Maggots often eat dead flesh.

methane (METH-ane)
Methane is a gas that has no smell or color but burns very easily. Cows produce methane when they pass gas.

microbes (MYE-krobez)
Microbes are very small living things. The human body is home to many microbes.

phosphate (FAHS-fate)
Phosphate is an organic compound often used in fertilizers. The island of Nauru has a lot of phosphate formed from ancient bird droppings.

LEARN MORE

BOOKS

Bathroom Readers Institute. *Uncle John's Bathroom Reader For Kids Only!* Ashland, OR: Portable Press, 2002.

Landstrom, Lee Ann, and Karen I. Shragg. *Nature's Yucky: Gross Stuff that Helps Nature Work.* Missoula, MT: Mountain Press, 2003.

WEB SITES

Visit our Web site for links about weird gross facts: **childsworld.com/links**

Note to Parents, Teachers, and Librarians: We routinely verify our Web links to make sure they are safe and active sites. So encourage your readers to check them out!

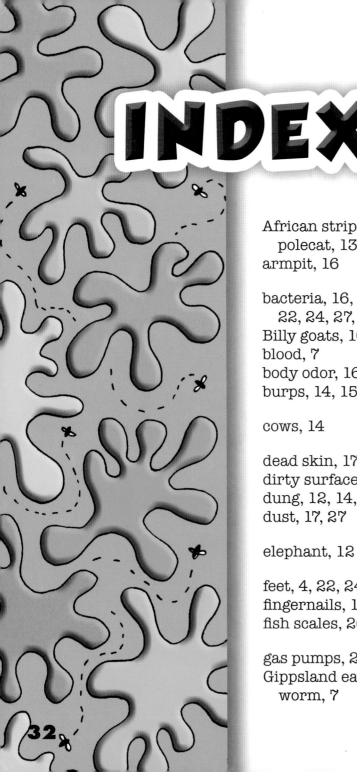

INDEX